T0208843

Poetic Pondering

A Transcendental Odyssey

BY

Stetson T. Thacker

iUniverse, Inc.
New York   Bloomington

Poetic Pondering
A Transcendental Odyssey

iUniverse books may be ordered through booksellers or by contacting:

iUniverse
1663 Liberty Drive
Bloomington, IN 47403
www.iuniverse.com
1-800-Authors (1-800-288-4677)

Because of the dynamic nature of the Internet, any Web addresses or links contained in this book may have changed since publication and may no longer be valid. The views expressed in this work are solely those of the author and do not necessarily reflect the views of the publisher, and the publisher hereby disclaims any responsibility for them.

ISBN: 978-1-4401-1809-8 (pbk)
ISBN: 978-1-4401-1810-4 (ebk)

Library of Congress Control Number: 2009920662

Printed in the United States of America

iUniverse rev. date:01/20/2009

ALONE A HEART

We once were very close
Not one thought, was bellicose
We were as good as jam and toast
We always had our love to boast

But swift came the change
Together, our hearts felt strange
Once the same but now were parted
Our thoughts and feelings were discarded

Thrown down into a pit less well
Drown out all feelings in a watery hell
And all that's left is desperate despair
She had the only heart that I could share

But I have no more desire to care
I have no more burdens I'm forced to bear
She was a leaden anchor to my soul
Never let me be completely whole

So I'm still here, a stand alone
No more feelings just flesh and bone
No catharsis to my tragic end
I no longer have a heart to spend

But I still have a tenacious will,
Infinite courage and daring skill
And now I'm free from my pain
I've washed away that tainted stain

I'll prosper so strong and free
Without someone controlling me
Because while alone, I have a heart
But with her, it was torn apart
We once were very close.

AMARANTHINE DIAMOND

Now, on display for its superiority,
Mounted on plush crushed velvet pillows,
Able to incite love like cupid's arrows,
Until brought forth into the world.

Now, worn upon a hand with dexterity,
Experiencing each exciting facet of life,
Enduring through frustration, pain, and strife,
Until the travail leaves it's marring mark.

Now, facing a laser blade with temerity,
Assured the result will be of betterment,
Distinguishing and empowering its
temperament.
Allowing the return to dignified pride.

Now, known for its invincibility,
And how its character withstood the fright,
With a tenacious amaranthine might,
Continuing a quest for shining excellence.

ANGELIC

Radiant star in the darkest night,
Sparkling diamond in the rough.
Shining like the brightest beacon,
Illuminating a life once so tough.

I desire to mirror this heavenly glow,
Display it for its owner's appreciation.
Or just to express thankfulness,
Because she evokes my admiration,

What providence was bequeathed to me?
To be gifted with someone so amazing,
An ethereal beauty, an angel of perfection, and
Guardian of my soul, she's done all the saving.

She's released me from my old prison,
Unbound me from my heavy chains
And like Daedalus, she gave me wings,
To fly away from my cruelest pains.

ASSUAGING SCORN

Scarlet love of pouring flame
Infernal river of passion
My audacious heart's devoid of shame

Even temerity can be rejected
Frozen in a crystal of solitude
In which only pain's reflected

And time may only thaw
That diamond of lonely souls
Until this, my heart's still raw

Bleeding from gaping orifices
From which my passion drains
Then sutured up with lustful kisses

At First Glance

It was like any morning.
Awake at the break of day.
Dressed in my clothes,
And then was on my way.

School sparked no intrigue,
Nothing special, nothing new,
But in night came change,
From a look came, came something true.

This glance exchanged,
Floored all senses,
Surrendered my heart,
On all pretenses.

But eyes fell away,
Like April rain.
Slightly abashed,
From thoughts so insane.

BEAUTIFUL GIRL

Beautiful girl, Beautiful girl
The only one to change my world
I know you feel the same as me
The greatest feeling that set us free

Beautiful girl, Beautiful girl
The only one to change my world
Kiss me once, and then kiss me twice
Nothing else but you, is just as nice

Beautiful girl, Beautiful girl
The only one to change my world
I fear your loss, so I hold you close
Walk with you down a romantic coast
Hand in hand and heart in heart
Always together and never apart

Beautiful girl, Beautiful girl
The only one to change my world
Come with me let's escape it all
I catch you if you slip and fall

BEYOND THE QUESTION

The answer is there.
On the brink of fruition,
Outside the capacity of possession,
Unlike a hot coal in hand,
Though the tortures are analogous.

Every attempt for explanation,
Drowns before its destination,
In the dark pools of ambiguity,
Portraying logic as gratuity.

That spot upon the map,
Is never really reached,
Its existence has been feigned,
Pretended, as if it were part of a play,
With only a basis in reality.

The veritable solution is ignorance:
The thesis for life and logic's concurrence,
It'll be written but never read,
And ultimately render curiosity dead.

BITTERSWEET

Bittersweet—
Is life and love
For life is bitter
And love is sweet
Dependent on each other
To stay functionally complete

Bondage

The soul inside my shell screams,
"Let me be free,
from this oppressive tyranny
that obstruct my sweetest dreams."

My shell ignores what my soul implore,
For base beings morality is a bore,
A mentally draining and burdening chore,
The exterior is always inferior to our cores.

BOUNDLESS LOVE

With my love so far from me
I cannot help but follow thee
So close my eyes and take my hand
Take me to my lover's land

Let's fly away, to another place
As long as I can see your face
It's our escape and sweet repose
A place that only our love knows

We'll settle down and make our home
Maybe a beach covered with sea foam
Or maybe we could live on top of the world
I don't mind as long as you're still my girl

Come back for me or I'll come along
I promise nothing will go wrong
Let's give hugs and a parting kiss
Because you'll be the only one I miss

But I'll still be with you, in your heart
Nothing can ever keep us apart
But still think of me and miss me too
And always know that I love you

BUTTERMILK TWIST

Buttermilk, buttermilk, buttermilk Twist
Jabbing right, crossing left
Dunking all over your head
Shame makes you wish you were dead
And that is all she said.

You got to recognize the
Fire in my eyes
I know I've got the drive,
The speed, the size.

Your game is fake, what the heck
Just like the jewels about your neck.
You don't got the passion,
For all this board crashing.

Don't make me say you don't got the moves
To make the game and the people groove.
For what I've got is unique
Your career outlook is severely bleak.
I know I broke your ankles and all you
Have to thank is….

Buttermilk, buttermilk, buttermilk Twist
Jabbing right, crossing left
Dunking all over your head
Shame makes you wish you were dead
And that is all she said.

This game is finished,
Your pride's diminished
But you're still talking smack
So I'll give you another whack
But you failed,
and now I've sailed

to the top and I'll never drop
that's why I pop all my shots
Never ever blocked
Cause I've got the twist and
You ain't never swift enough to stop it.

I'm just too smooth,
For all your grooves
And your shoes and all the
Other playin' foos
Who think they can beat me and my feet
That are sweet and never cheat.

I'm the chosen one,
I got all the fun
When beating you
A cheating foo
So go home,
And tell all your homies
About it, shout it,
Cause the 'Buttermilk Twist' is in town.

Buttermilk, buttermilk, buttermilk Twist
Jabbing right, crossing left
Dunking all over your head
Shame makes you wish you were dead
And that is all she said.

CATACLYSMIC

Jensen: Fifteen by fifteen space,
      Is all I have to navigate.
      At thirty-five on route
      To save some lives
      I miss my wife,
      A light-year away
      We humans can go anywhere
      How did I end up here?
      Oh no, What was that?
      I've heard a stowaway.
      Quick, I have my gun,
      I'll save my life, so ripe and young.

Cassandra: No, I mean no harm,
      I'm only eight,
      With a dying wish,
      For one last look
      At my brother's face.

Jensen: We're on a EDS
      Does this make sense?
      That means you go,
      And I will stay.
      Someone has to save the day.
      But this just is to simple and severe,
      I'm torn between you and me,
      Along with another thirty.

Cassandra: It's alright, I understand.
      But let me make one demand.
      Save my brother from disease,
      And the rest of them, if you please.
      I'm not worth,
      The sum of thirty.
Jensen: Don't speak like that,

Because you are in fact
Worth any sacrifice.
You remind me of my own,
I would die for her,
So take all controls,
Don't let this mission fail.

Cassandra: I denounce what you say,
For losing you, Is just the same.
Bypass the rules,
We'll fly with danger,
We'll make death a forgotten
stranger.
It will work,
Just dare to trust.
All that physics stuff,
Is one big fuss.

Jensen: I presume this obviates my goodbye,
Our only option is to try.
So gaze upon the sky,
And draw from it audacity.
Together we fight,
To stave off disconsolation.
We might be forgotten,
But were not forsaken,
For if death shall come,
Our courage will not be taken.

CHERISHED

Stone has withered,
Trees have died,
But my love for her,
Has stayed alive.
Armor tarnished,
Battles lost,
But for her,
Who cares the cost.

CHRISTMAS FAMILY

Every house is adorned in a seasonal array
Algid weather reminds us that Christmas is here to stay
Merry melodies are sung by carolers caroling place to place
Not a single missing smile on any frostbitten face
Every home radiates a cheerful Yuletide glow;
A perfect amount, preventing the melting of Noel's snow
By the raging fire: a Christmas tree, the epitome of Christmas cheer,
Underneath, presents sleep waiting for avid children to appear
Rouse them from their sheets of holiday wrapping paper
Allowing children's anxious spirits to relax and taper
Excitement then flows from their tiny bodies in appreciation
Every family member thankful for Christ's creation
So off to Church to thank the liberal lord
And abate the ardent youth until they're bored
Then slip into their dreams, to reclaim their forfeited slumber
Until, they're awoken by the aroma of burning lumber
Warming the brumal air for those beside the fireside
Awaiting the feast prepared specifically for the Yuletide
Once festivities end a blissful somnolence reciprocates
An exemplary example of how a Christmas loving family celebrates!

COMPASSION

TO: a bereaved friend who has suffered the loss of a
parent.

The wound there to see
has provoked kindness within
to allay cruel pain
clean and dress, prevent scarring
return your soft perfection

Cousin To Little Cousin

Well, Kennae, I'll tell you:
Life for me hasn't been a down mattress.
It's had bugs in it,
And lumpy bumps,
And holes in the sheets,
And dark sweat stains all over from—
Stress
But still every night
I've slept sound on it,
And dreamt in its wake,
And curled up in it warmth,
Sometimes ignoring the loud popping,
Of springs as I roll over.
So Kennae, don't lose your courage.
Don't chose to lay awake
'Cause you find it less mysterious.
Don't be a coward now—
For I still sleep alright,
And I'm still dreaming,
And life for me hasn't been a down mattress.

Cutie Pie

She's just my cutie pie
That's lost her alibi
And I won't let her spirit die
She makes us all look shy

Nor sunset nor sunrise
Are as beautiful as her eyes
The laws of nature they defy
Absolutely no one can deny

Skin as smooth as piano keys
Tastes as good as honey made from bees
Always gives me wobbly knees
And I'm the only one she sees

You only have to look inside
To fall in love with her every side
There's nothing that I need to hide
The love we have won't ever abide

DESTINED LOVER

The stars align,
She becomes mine.
Our eyes meet,
Hearts skip a beat.

She walks to accost,
I freeze like flowers in frost.
She speaks words of love,
Words directly from above.

I feel at ease,
With my heart pleased.
I know she's mine,
God sent that sign.
When stars align,
She's forever mine.

DIVERSITY

Diversity comes in every shape
Oblong here but square there
Many fear and hate it
But I wish it present everywhere

It allows ingenuous expression
And fosters the beginnings of empathy
Lets us see the other perspective
In which true diversity has our sympathy

Still some prefer things flat
So they miss the scenic mountains
Their just daunted by a mixed society
And resolve to drink from separate fountains

Their living prairie is absurdity
No satisfaction can be found in things the same
Lets open up their narrow minds
And give diversity a different name

Who will be our Moses, and
Lead us away from similarity,
Teach us differences are valuable
So diversity can thrive in our posterity

DON'T LOOK BACK

Walked a lonely street,
On the broken path between my feet.
To step past your blame,
And to reclaim my fame,

All alone at the top,
'Cause this tune won't spot,
And I can feel the beat,
That saves me from defeat.

So don't look back,
'Cause I won't be there,
You're out of luck,
'Cause I'm everywhere.

Don't fight what's right,
My streak can't end,
'Cause I can reach out of reach,
Been farther than God's been.

Doubt

is this what is real?

evanescent certainty

from murky puddles

that frequent holes on the road

Consuming the careless feet

ENDEAVOR FOR SUCCESS

What is that soft and fuzzy light?
Dimly gleaming through endless darkness,
As bright as any other just forced to brave the night.

Illuminates a path severely less tread,
Because it's sown with ambiguity,
Into noble fabric with a needle point of dread.

An annoying dogged and uphill trail,
The steepest of them all,
The most tenacious brave its slope to no avail,

Only those who swell proud with passion
Conquer this insurmountable journey
And never fail to do it an awe-inspiring fashion

But besmirched their names become,
Slandered with notorious conceit,
Condemned by most, yet worshipped by some.

That fraction is all that is important,
Made up of only the special chosen,
Who still receive banter from all remaining mordant.

Eternal Struggle

It's hard to live in pain,
When all you see is freedom.
A king imprisoned in a cage,
But left to see his kingdom.

A torture so unbearable,
It fosters great disdain.
For things I once desired,
And hoped and prayed to gain.

Every drop of sweat I spent,
Undoubtedly are saturated in contempt.
All my efforts I now repent.
And wish them fantasies I dreamt.

Why fight this battle any longer?
Why raise the flags again?
I do it to get stronger,
And for the heart and souls of men.

EVERY MORNING

Every Morning
At the break of dawn
I Awaken
To my loved one's song

Every Morning
I think of her
Reflect on thoughts
Only my dreams can spur

Every Morning
Shining bright and warm
I'm flooded her love
Like a thunder storm

Every Morning
I live again
To pursue my dream
That has always been

EXISTENCE

A cry, a break, a sudden stop,
Through unknown to a frozen stop.
So cold, so stark, a dismal end,
Grows a beginning of sorrow's blend.
Of hate, of love, and heaven above,
Seize the fears in a wrathful glove.
So fight, so resist, a fading destiny,
Allow immured spirits to be set free.
To live, to seek, for some content,
Before the last ounce of life is spent.
So bloom, so thrive, seize the moment,
Factor in the last component.
To equip, to ready, for any mission,
And have a final act of contrition,
For sin, for wrong, and all damnation,
To give existence some sensation.
Don't stop, don't wait, no time to think,
This is fulfillment on the brink,
Of disaster, of tragedy, of no avail,
Another chance for hope to fail.
Say hello, say goodbye, take a rest,
This is existence at its best.

FADING FOLIAGE

Suspended for an evanescent epoch,
Bathing beautifully in the autumn breeze
Flutters free foliage with graceful ease.
A butterfly robbed of its sovereignty.

This precious, precious moment fades,
With the leaf meeting cold, grassy ground,
Making a sonorously deafening sound,
A profound and ephemeral note.

Reduced to a pigmented, deciduous carnage,
The loss of a great, vivacious beauty,
Evidently explains life's sacred duty:
Appreciate each passing piece.

FICKLE LIMITS

Limits don't govern all
Some have a sovereign spirit
Gravity makes us humans fall
But still lets angels fly
Why ,to us, does gravity apply?
No learned logic can descry;
Explanation for those who ground defy.
"Injustice" the unprivileged fervently decry

FORSAKEN

Why have you flown,
So far from me,
I despise myself,
For loving thee.

My soul lies destroyed,
A dismal hollow shell,
Forsaken by its only need.
A hostage to feelings that can't be freed.

Despair I scream,
For all to hear,
Licentious nature,
Is what I fear.

It's bestowed on me,
This incumbent grudge,
Condemned to hate,
And to always prejudge.

I detest my fate,
To be abandoned,
I reject this hate,
And will stay standing.

I'll swallow my revulsion,
In Fate's loathing face.
Suspend all malevolence,
In every place.

FRUSTRATION IN HAND

I grasp my hand within the sand.
I plunge it deep into unknown depth,
Then draw it up and tighten my hold.
My tightening hold just increases the flow
Of sand, that's now streaming through my hand,
I might as well be grasping at water
But I'm forced to try this folly again,
And only apprehensions in my fingers,
As I look at the warm sparkling sand,
Whatever I attain will inevitably drain,
Rain between my fingers back onto the beach,
And my anguish is evolving into shame,
My shame wont dissipate until it becomes pain,
I can never bare the slightest once of agony
It's the softest spot in my armor; an Achilles' heel,
A cavity within my hard and valiant enamel,
That emptiness has been predestined to fill,
And no travail can help mitigate that hollow hole.

FUNCTIONING LOVE

I'm just waiting for the answer to the sine,
And hoping that you'll be my valentine.
We're more complicated than a logarithm,
But still our desire remains in a good rhythm.
Our love's as beautiful as a quadratic function.
At Valentine's Day will be our crucial junction,
But still our passion's restricted by asymptotes,
But since we have no holes there's still hope.
Our feelings compound like interest;
Continuously if we do request.
Were like conjugates of each other.
Once our equations factored it equals love.
As complex as we are we remain rational,
In our domain we stay together often too emotional,
Though we'll be linear without points of inflection,
And if you'll be my valentine we've obviated correction.

GLORY

It sits upon a throne of veneration:
A position that makes others jealous.
For it's the focal point of celebration,
Without it we've destroyed appreciation.

Our hearts palpitate because it has force,
The effable energy that intrigue the zealous:
Loads the bandwagon on glory's course,
Explains its nature and recondite source.

Splendor is an ornamental majestic place,
That manifests itself only there:
The ethereal point between earth and space,
That coalesces together with divine grace.

Although its heaven this is indulgence,
But maybe seductive glory's impossible to bear,
And still act simply with great prudence:
It's a potion of powerful potence.

Enjoy each drop but don't be consumed,
Because glory is just greed perfumed,
And dressed in the vestments of virtue:
A dichotomy for our minds to construe.

HEART CONTRIVED

She looks into my eyes,
My heart immured starts to cry,
With all the lies locked inside,
And all the love that's failed and died.
Christen me her faithful lover,
No more lies and no more others,
She might not know it now,
But my heart will surely allow,
Her to share a spot,
Atop my heart's contrived plot.

HEAVENLY BEAUTY

Your eyes they tell a story

Of all our love and all our glory

Beauty like a sunrise

Is why I stare at your eyes

Your smile shows of bliss

Right after every kiss

I always feel I miss

The sweetness of your lips

Baby soft and velvet felt

Your skin, my heart it melts

Stretched across my loving dream

Perfect is how you always seem

HERMETIC SOLITUDE

He rides in the darkest night
Like shadows on the window sills
But in his eyes shines the brightest light;
A piercing visage that gives us chills

He is always seen solemn and alone
But never in essence is he ever seen
With his gaunt face all skull and bone
So by his countenance we judge him mean

His skin is pale, tallow, and vapid
Yet unwrinkled or marred by any scar
He's never intimate, his nature's just too rapid
Thus, seems an apparition when gazed on from afar

His demeanor is steadfast and unchanging:
A marble sculpture of a constant hero
That's completely invulnerable to deranging
Consequently ambivalence labels him a zero

To him perception holds no weight
He already bears the weight of many things
His incumbent duties never do abate
The evident agony obviously stings

But real self-pity he still denies
He has refused to break and crumble
He has become intolerant of simple lies
He's resolved to just be quiet and stay humble

Composure in him is a being of its own
Resilient enough to never falter

Unfortunately, his spirits haven't ever flown
Because then, his composure, it would alter

The gravity upon him hasn't made him hostile
Society is something he absorbs peculiarly
Digesting all the world with the strongest bile
Prevents himself from perceiving the world as hostile

HONEST PIRATE

Fidelity to honest piracy
Is his largest irony
And an eccentricity
And not always, simplicity,

He winks,
He smiles,
He shots his gun,
It's not for fun

Its life
His strife
He's the only one
Whose honesty is matched by none
His comrades plunder
Their lives asunder

He still finds treasures
And enjoys the pleasures
Of sailing the seven seas
Or drinking rum under palm trees

Inspired by Jack Sparrow played by Johnny Depp

Hope And You And Me

Luck has fed and nursed my lonely heart,
And saved me tenderly from a cynical fate.
Then envy tried to severe our bond apart,
But our feelings conquered that vengeful hate.

We now sit on our happy thrones,
King and Queen of our auspicious predestination.
Still we must face bitter sticks and stones,
But with one hopeful and romantic expectation.

Storms will inevitably float our way,
We will endure them patiently together,
Binding closer in the ensuing fray,
Emerging stronger to spite that weather.

I vow my heart is yours for spending,
I pray this happiness is never-ending.

I Count The Steps

I count the steps,
The distance to,
The time when it was me and you,
-So
-Far

-Gone

If every time,
And every place,
Were given up and lost in space,
-Where'd
-I

-go

Life's been spent,
And life's been lost,
I do it all at any cost,
-What's
-the

-price

I'll fight for you,
You'll fight for me,
We'll regain our serenity,
-When
-it's

-done

I have to tell,
I have to scream,
This is what its like to dream,
-I
-love

-you

All I am,
All I was
Is all for you, just because;
-You're
-the

-one

I Love You

I love you so much
I cry when it rains
But bury distress my love
It's not in the slightest pain

And every time I close my eyes
I see your face on mine
Locked in the most loving embrace
That absolutely nothing can erase

Our bond was grown from the strongest seed
And our love will flourish through word and
deed
I'd give up anything and even bleed
Just to attend to her every need

In The Skies

Sweetest blooms in the Autumnal breeze,
Whose roots grow strong in times of need,
Albeit that tender breeze is fleeting,
Remember that scent before it leaves.

Beauty is beneath the leaf blanketed ground,
Awaiting the call of the vernal spirits,
Crisp air allays those spirits' fervor,
Sates desire and preserves perfection.

It's eternal as the heavens are,
Radiant as the stars that dot the sky.
The aesthetic designs of idealistic deities,
Who believe mortality intensifies our fantasies.

Because love conquers death in battle,
It is knighted by immortals in paradise,
Its essence there hides so cravenly,
The gaze of death only provokes bravery.

The blood lost notarizes a heart's passion,
Every open wound is evidence,
From which buds the veins of love:
The universal purpose revered by those above.

INSIPID JARGON

The cliché remarks of every day,
Paint the world in total gray.
Overwhelm brilliance with banality,
In the timeless struggle for tranquility,
Hypocrisy becomes an unchallenged law,
And ingenuousness is a tragic flaw.
Honor and bravery are long neglected;
The era in which ipseity is corrected.
An aftermath of a dreary platitude,
Patterned out in lines of latitude,
Predictable in use and meaning,
Manifestations should incite immediate gleaning.
To refine the metal that tips the arrow,
With emotive words only meant to harrow,
Pierce the mind to keep its thoughts neoteric.
Mystery within the words is purposefully esoteric.

Last Time

Last time I saw you,
You turned away.

Last time I missed you,
You caused my tears.

Last time I hurt you,
You forgave my sins.

Last Time I knew you,
You stole my heart.

Last time I was with you,
I got lost in your eyes.

Last time I loved you,
You loved me back.

Last time I check,
I was still yours.

LIFE'S A TWO SIDED SPHERE

Life's a two sided sphere.
Upon each new facet,
The same textures appear.
An infinite smoothness,
Intensifies a flagrant fear,
Of universal congruity;
Vanishes hope of being sincere.
Evaporates like the boiling water in our minds

LOST AND FOUND

Around a wrist,
In style and bliss,
Fell between a kiss,
Left for none to miss.

Past up and treaded on,
All beauty forever gone,
Rescued from the earth,
Given hope in rebirth.

Strapped back across,
Saved from eternal loss,
Given a new refuge,
Safe from Lonely's deluge.

LOVE

It is in the small things we see it.
A fleeting look of passion
that stabs you like Cupid shoots his arrows.
It's in the first time someone hugs you tight
like the warmth in summer embracing sunshine.
And while you grow so does your love:
A young sapling grown strong and solid,
Your branches ready to reach and learn
to grasp the branches of another tree,
And soon you'll become intertwined,
like pieces of string spun into yarn
that will bind your hearts forever.

Later,
If your amour's ardent and burgeoning
you might accidentally run it a stormy battlefield
where emotional bullets rain on your soft skull,
And every battle is essential but so is sacrifice,
Sometimes losing is not an end but a beginning:
You are a phoenix rising from your ashes.
For love is a simple thing with wings
That glides over the heads of roses
and settles comfortably in the dandelions.

Later,
If you take love for granted it seems to disappear:
Lemonade evaporating on a sultry summer day,
That could have assuaged your zealous thirst,
But now has floated to oblivion because of your neglect.
So don't forget to keep your feelings dancing,
Sharpen them as frequently as a butcher sharpens knives.
Cultivated your ardor by planting new seeds in your garden,
Show them sunshine and quench their avid thirst,
Treat them with care and despair when they fall to the garden bed.
For love is like stained glass precious and pretty but fragile.

Later,
You understand that it is in your gardens and forests,
Your heart now wants to share its treasures,
Teach it to the others absolutely free of charge,
So you have written your passionate book,
And its time to let the reader read and enjoy,
The love you have written will live on,
Even when your internal light's extinguished,
and placed inside the ground to rot,
What you gave still walks alive and makes the world brighter.

LOVE'S ENCOUNTER

I'M AT A GAME,
THIS DAY IS PLAIN.
BUT I SEE
NEW EYES AT ME,
THEY SPEAK A LIFE.
PENETRATE LIKE A KNIFE.
EAT MY SOUL,
AND DEVOUR IT WHOLE.
BUT TIME STANDS STILL,
AND WILL STAY UNTIL,
MY LOVE'S EYES,
WILL MAKE ME CRY,
ALL MY FEELING,
TO START RE-HEALING,
MY PRIDE AND COURAGE,
TO PREVENT DISCOURAGE,
OF HEARTS PLEASURES
AND LOVE'S TREASURE.

MISSED

It's always there,
Like the sun,
When you get up in the mourning,
Or the moon,
When you sink,
Into a tempting dream.

I miss her,
Every moment,
She's not around,
I hope she's made it home,
Safe and sound.

I miss that smile,
Her beauty,
The taste of a kiss,
Her presence is what I miss.

My heart will race,
When I know she's near.
I am happier,
Than I can appear.

Never Let You Go

Infectious beauty ensnares my soul

Taken a grip that won't let go

It's held me here from then 'til now

Endured all resistance and I know how

A vice grip like this, has a heavenly
source

One that has saved me from a desolate
course

I return that grip and hold on tight

To preserve a light in the darkest night

Neither dreams to loosen hold

For forever and a day I've told

I will never let you go

I will never let you go

NIGHTMARE

Speak soft, not to hurt the ear

The words you speak are too severe,

My feeble mind is utterly vulnerable

Weakening with each deafening syllable,

I can endure no longer, no farther should I tread

I'm succumbing to desires, that are safer in my head,

Escape is just a wish, lofty optimistic dreams

I live within a nightmare, filled with frightful screams

NUMB

I can't feel the rain,
Upon my back.
For I've lost a soul,
And lost my track.
Winter's chills hollow my bones,
Bringing despair in dreary tones,
As I slump along a vacant course,
I'm struck down by a mournful force.
Snares me up and runs me through.
Removes my faith like a broken
screw,
That's been torn out for later use,
To nail a coffin around me and you.
As barren as the Tundra,
I lay an apathetic corpse,
Wanting for the day,
I learn to feel remorse.

Nursing Hope

Once to the pallid flower I flew
To nurture this diseased rose of life
I approached with cautious care
And gazed softly onto its petals,
Disfigured by plague of wilting
And devoid of old, florid, flare
But dignity still, fills its base and stem
And hold this rose up in resilience
Through climates impossible for any to bear
Which berate this withered yet constant blossom,
And when its flatten to the flowerbed,
Abjectly displayed for all to stare,
The roots adamantly cling to earth
So when spring comes it can lift its head
To absorb the sun's reviving glare.

Ode To Love

No such thing,
Can rival this,
Make you sigh,
And love to kiss.
So hold it dear,
And don't let go,
Fight sword and spear,
To preserve the hope,
Look upon starry skies,
To find meaning in life,
Written in the constellations,
Shining through the darkest nights,
It lights the path
For those who seek companions,
Opens wide a door,
Like a river in a canyon.
It gives a purpose,
To those with none,
To beseech the hand,
Of an important one.

"Our Story"

I was swept away in a glance,
Stunned by its profound power,
Aided my timid heart's growth of bravery,
To leave myself unguarded to chance.
But salacious whispered insults follow,
Their incessant envy is a deadly sin,
There countenance a livid green,
Their hearts are sadly hollow,
Although some infuse me with worry,
Try to injure you each moment,
That I cannot be your savior,
Minor tragedy in our romantic story.
But happiness fills every chapter,
Every word redolent of your smile,
Saved by eyes as a memorable image,
Your soul is my cordial captor.
Drowns hope to its nadir.

One word apart,
Divides the thought,
Affords new wisdom,
That Time has bought.

ONE WORD

One word in the night,
Is just a whisper by day,
The impact resounds,
And silenced the fray.

One word of Love,
Beckons crafty Cupid,
Lets loose the arrows,
That make wise men stupid.

One word of spite,
Pierces the heart,
With blazing blades,
That Malice sharpened apart.

One word of hope,
Illuminated the dark,
Guided the hopelessly lost,
With the songs of the Lark.

One word of pain,
In a child's tear,
Wells up and flows,
Drowns hope to its nadir.

One word apart,
Divides the thought,
Affords new wisdom,
That Time has bought.

PAIN OF BEAUTY

Every season has a lesson,
Taught by the professor,
Who dwells upon the sky.

Pain is the coldest product
And beauty may be its price.
So as to see the starry night.

That night will lengthen,
Algid air will bite your skin,
Leaving you in burning agony,
But stifled by each piece of heaven,
That falls frozen from the sky.

Each piece an individual,
With a unique personality,
That weathers winter's constancy.

Frozen still in descension,
The moment is eternal,
Inevitably melting to its destiny

Frozen flakes have fallen,
Each a piece in the whitest quilt,
That covers barren thoughts,
A warmly effective coat,
To stop the painful cold.

PARADISIACAL REVERIE

The sun descends below the sea
Those last rays were left for me
Where I'm nestled in the cooling sand;
Adhering to the skin I've tanned

Now all that's left is starry sky
The type even cynics can't deny.
Moon glow makes the shoreline shine
Accentuating the beach's exquisite design

Palm trees burst forth from the shore
Underneath are coconuts it once bore
The tide comes to wash beach serene
And wake me from this pleasant dream

PASSION EPOCH

I was impassive once,
In another time.
When I look back,
I see my crime.

But forget what's past,
It's been replaced.
My heart's encased,
By a love that lasts.

I fell so fast,
And almost crashed,
But I'm content,
With my present.

My passion's Epoch,
Has everlasting luck.
Never ceasing to bring surprise,
Avoiding any insidious demise.

Poems Of Time

Poems in essence tell of the time.
An era encoded in each stanza,
Its people's thoughts within each rhyme
Each poem has a unique face,
But map an epoch all in same method.
From one to twelve, date, time, and place,
They're the clocks of culture:
An esoteric timepiece only for certain societies.
They give history authentic texture.

PREDICTABLY WRONG

If life and behavior were constant
And all our thoughts the same
We'd be drawn out on a map
That'd be supine and never change

We would never feel surprised
Certainty would oppress our minds
Reducing us the pawns of the game
Maneuvered to our predictable destinations

Our emotion would be controlled
Never volatile or susceptible to provoking
Of course we'd anticipate the provocations
And then react according to what was foretold

Change is a foreign and abstract idea
One we sorrowfully misconstrue
We believe it present in our world
Unaware that our assumptions are untrue

REAL COOL

The celebrities
In the lap of luxury

We live High. We
dress fly. We

smell nice. We
wear ice. We

age slow. We
like show. We

set trend. We
don't end.

REVIVAL

I feel my perfect day drawing to its close,
The sun has been descending,
To shade the wilted rose.

The darkness is a blind solitude,
With only a memory of the day's beauty,
To buttress the crumbling wall of fortitude.

In the Lunar rays I lay prostrate,
Depressed by the desperation,
Flowing in my tears of hate.

Warmth and light aren't forever lost,
They're buried in mounds of animosity,
Until the light rises against the morning frost.

The young hours may still appear bleak,
But the sun's an auspicious sign,
Awakes beings from their nadir

SALVATION

In heaven lies one salvation,
The finish line of consolation,
Marking the end of damnation,
Abjure the oath of condemnation
Divine life beats on Earth,
And strives within purity,
All blinded in holy sensation,
Seduced by the melody of consecration,
Reduced to provincial desecration,
And the blossom of evil elation
Our heaven is a contract
Nullified by only lies,
Suffer and endure temptation,
Watch the grotesque transformation,
Inside the dark soul in dilation,
The deleterious eye of adulation,
Because nature is the strongest,
Let it guide your heart.

SOLITUDE

Solitude, the seed alone
That strips away all flesh from bone,
Bores inside to leave a scar
Sometimes abated, but never far.

Is lonely considered safe?
An alternate ending or better place.
In this event I cry dissent
Love forever wins true assent.

Separate and lost the throngs depart
With broken hearts so torn apart.
Dreams destroyed with hearts so starved
Riddled with the scars that lovely carved.

STARSTRUCK

I only once have had the luck
To be the one to be starstruck
By the loveliest being to ever live
To her, all my heart I wish to give

She's stunning, striking, and brilliant
With her heart and mind resilient
She's so shockingly amazing
Looking at her is like star gazing

It was all in one look
In which, my heart, she took
And threw me to the skies
When there I saw those eyes

Those shining hazel spheres
That pierce me like sharpened spears
So I can completely see
How starstruck she's made me

Streetside individuality

1. When those who look
2. Still dread to see
3. And when their doors are closed
4. I wander out to observe
5. Lonely and barren dreams,
6. That sometimes waltz along the sidewalks
7. Always glimmering in the streetlights
8. Inevitably they're forced to halt their journeys
9. To nurse their sickly hearts, so full of worries

10. Every night their numbers dwindle;
11. Who brave the night with me,
12. Former drifters have found comforting conformity
13. Feeling content in their heart-warming houses
14. Where they're free to rest their heads
15. Clear out their fears of misery;
16. But with their agony goes their introspection
17. And without reflection their cannot be progression
18. A lonely lull is all that will be left for eternity.

19. They sleep, let their time tick away
20. 'Til every last hand has struck
21. The passive and differential hours
22. Where the world's free to run itself
23. And the time's not decided, by its winder
24. But by the banal gears and gizmos
25. Which cannot be altered by any person
26. Now that we've lost our former reference
27. The sorry contribution of the former dreamers

28. So docility's been established, none will disagree
29. They've complied to sell away their destinies
30. Sacrificed their old provocative originalities

31. That challenged the values of sanctity,
32. Our campaign's been compromised by grotesque conformity,
33. All of its unifying lies that cajole away the cold,
34. Chills no longer remind us of the reasoning of old
35. That used to preserve each idiosyncratic personality
36. A sanctuary from our clandestinely clouded reality

STRONG OF FEELING

I know I'm strong of feeling,
But for adoration,
I have been short in dealing,
My hope is felicitation,
At the conclusion of your healing.

I see your figure at the distant pier,
The ocean winds wrench my heart,
Because I wish that you were here,
Instead divided, an ocean apart,
Yet still our hearts seem very near.

You appear to me in dream,
As if you were surreal,
Unbelievable how my heart can scream,
That in earnest is how I feel,
While touching skin as soft as cream
Reality is the way things seem.

SUNSHINE PETAL

Brilliance flashes in your saffron complexion,
But this brilliance is worn demurely:
A star dressed in velvety gentle glow,
For its still algid and the season's early.

There is no roof upon our sky.
Don't let your roots cement you down,
Stiffen your stem flaunt your petals,
Wear them as a queen wears a crown.

Grasp the sunshine within your petals,
For then within me happiness will fill;
Sweet aromas proclaim the story,
Of the sweetest vernal daffodil.

TEARDROPS

In happiness of sorrow,
They won't be here tomorrow
Stream down your pretty face
Only there for me to erase

My wish is for them to disappear
With any hate or fear
I want only a happy bliss
That all the sad tears will miss

No tears will fall
From your face at all
All teardrops will dry
And no one will ever need to cry

THE ABSURD WORLD

Tomorrow-tomorrow or day to day
Confusion throws solidity in disarray
Confounded nightmares impair recollection
And obviate requisites of reflection

THE SEVEN KISSES OF LIFE

Life is a pair of lips,
That are blessed with a new kiss,
From the different lips of life.
The first is the kiss of life,
Which brings all people into this world.
The embrace of discovery succeeds,
The endearment of birth,
This kiss is a breath of fresh air,
To the wandering spirit within,
Subsequent to discovery comes love,
The lips of love catch us all,
And throw us into a bonfire of emotion,
Twirling us round n' round in burning passion,
Until the kiss of parenthood comes pecking,
To fill our cavity with a fourth set of lips,
Parenthood the experience of a life time of a life time,
Contributed to brushing lips with knowledge,
And the elusive fugitive wisdom,
These e lips lament over world crises,
And chew through books as beavers chew trees,
But having wisdom on the pallet,
Can only help us discover that we're unwise,
And thus we meet the lips of reflection,
Absorbing us back in time,
From creation till now
Reflections is like the sweetest candy,
But it leaves only one aftertaste
Final departure, the kiss of death

THE SPACE BETWEEN

The space between,
Our lovely lips,
Is just a breath,
After a loving kiss.

The Space between,
What's right and wrong,
Has been written down,
In every song.

The space between,
My heart and hers,
Is not but a touch,
That love incurs.

The space between,
Her Thoughts and mine,
Are just a barrier,
Of our design.

The space between,
The start and end,
Is between land and sky,
Without limits to comprehend.

Trick Or Treat

It's the night.
We're out again.
Drowning in illusion.
Bag in hand.

Fear in veins.
Hearts skip like sprites.
Guided by darkness.
Lost to magic.

Time dissolve.
Arms become burdened branches.
Sagging with despair.
Below our smiling faces.

Voracious appetites
relieve our tiny arms.
Satiate our pith
with lovely happiness.

VICTORIOUS DAYDREAM

During the most intolerable and,
Boring of classes I find my young mind
Wandering off to the baseball finals,
A place some day I ardently wish to be.
A chance to stand on that six inch high hill
Above the diamond with all the eyes on me,
And my uniform stitched with the word "Redskins",
Blazing brightly across my tired heavy chest
My hat tilted slightly to the left and,
Tight over my eyes to hide my shaking heart.
The roar of the crowd hits like a tidal wave,
But instead of overwhelming me, I absorb it.
Then channel that energy though my taut body,
Exciting my soul like pure adrenaline
excites the muscles of every physical being.
I step on the flat rubber at my feet
And look at my catcher to receive signals.
I taste salty dirt stinging my raw lips.
I'm locked in. I know what I want to throw.
I get my desired sign and give a nod
Then twirl the ball and grasp a four-seem grip,
I begin my wind up and lift my leg high,
Let it land solidly in the dirty ground.
Aggressively my tense arm lets the pitch fly.
"Strike three" exclaims the enormous black umpire.
We are victors, and jubilation fills in me,
But then my pertinent teacher jolts me awake
From my simple sweet midday reverie.

What is Love?

Is love just capricious adoration?
A temporal, evanescent feigned sensation,
Can it be blind and unquestionable?
Or is it meant to be testable?

Who decides when love will call?
What if you never fall in love at all?
When can affection ever be trusted?
Why can true feelings be adjusted?

When someone's feelings lie behind a curtain
It's impossible to ever be for certain
If everything that was felt was actual
Because love in any form is never factual

Does love have to make us contrite
Are these the feelings, love will incite,
An amalgam of antipathy, and hate.
Who holds the answer to this debate?

Enlightening Night

Before I read "Night" by Eli Wiesel in my eighth grade English class I perceived the world as small. My weltanschauung was provincial because I egotistically related everything to myself; I was the vain Narcissus who spurned the love of Echo because I was too naïve to see the world resonating with issues of higher importance than issues concerning myself. However, unlike Narcissus, I was able to repent by expanding my weltanschauung instead of being condemned to be entranced by the reflection of my provincial ways. Eli Wiesel's poignant memoir about the agony and travail he endured and overcame in Nazi death camps enlightened me to a world full of people who have suffered in almost unimaginable ways.

Mrs. Frye was my eighth grade English teacher. As unorganized, absent-minded, and eccentric as she was, her passion, intelligence, and diligence made her one of the best teachers I have ever been graced with. She was the one to introduce me to Night. Upon my completion of Night (which I finished in a day because I could not wrench my eyes from the pages) I became disillusioned, melancholy, and guilt ridden. A tornado of emotions divested me of my egotistical assumption and perspective and left me a painful emptiness. My only solace was my awareness of a world that stretched far beyond the wake of my shadow.

In retrospect, my initial position was beyond vulnerable: I was a little corvette smashed by a semi-truck of disillusionment. However, I could not simply replace myself like one can replace a car: I had to rebuild piecemeal with the wisdom I had gained from Wiesel's book. I am still under construction but I have learned that to improve society and the world around me I must excel. From Wiesel's memoir, I concluded that I must try to solve problems that plague the world: AIDS pandemics in Africa, genocide in Bosnia , world hunger, etc. This is a lofty goal; however as I have grown and garnered pieces of wisdom, I realized solving a major world problem is not a necessary end. Instead, the perspective that the world extends beyond one's own problems and then acting properly upon that philosophy is necessary to improving as an individual, which consequently improves the world. Every society needs people who work assiduously and sacrifice for others instead of pursuing their own ends: every little action of altruism and generosity matters. Thus, I resolved to alter my motives to a far greater cause then myself: society and posterity.

Altruism is said to be a product of wisdom that one gains through experience that giving happiness to others reciprocates unto the giver and is advantageous to society holistically because an acts of kindness have the tendency to become contagious. Thus, I aspire to be truly altruistic; however I have not yet brought this aspiration to fruition. But I still cherish the consciousness I have of the need to contribute to the world and step outside the provincial bubble of my existence to aide others. "Night" was my guide to a more expansive world-view; it laid the foundation for who I am today and who I aspire to be.

Stetson Thacker January 2009

Author's Biography

Stetson Thacker is a gifted 17 year-old high school junior who has been writing poetry since elementary school. He has won poetry contests and has published in literary magazines and was the art editor for his Cuyahoga Heights High School literary magazine **Ephemeris**. The name "Stetson" evokes the image of a rugged American Western cowboy. His mother muses that she picked his name 'out of hat' also noting that he shares his name with Stetson University. He is a strong 3 sport Varsity athlete who has a poet's heart, an insightful mind, and quiet but charming and genuinely altruistic nature. His vast interests are reflective of a Renaissance man. He is an honor student in Science, Mathematics, French, English and History. He is a class leader, captain of the Academic Challenge team, city wide National Vocabulary Contest winner, a state qualifer for "Power of the Pen", community volunteer and founded his school's "Junior Statesman Foundation" chapter of which he serves as President. He can usually be found with a book in hand and his young memoir is based on a book.